T0402880

THE TENNESSEE
TITANS

BY ALICIA Z. KLEPEIS

EPIC

BELLWETHER MEDIA ★ MINNEAPOLIS, MN

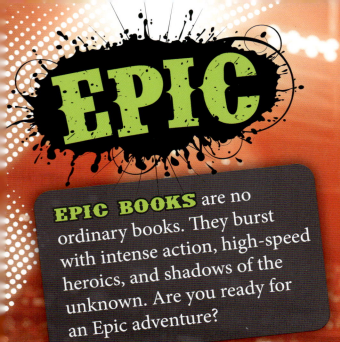

EPIC

EPIC BOOKS are no ordinary books. They burst with intense action, high-speed heroics, and shadows of the unknown. Are you ready for an Epic adventure?

This edition first published in 2024 by Bellwether Media, Inc.

No part of this publication may be reproduced in whole or in part without written permission of the publisher. For information regarding permission, write to Bellwether Media, Inc., Attention: Permissions Department, 6012 Blue Circle Drive, Minnetonka, MN 55343.

Library of Congress Cataloging-in-Publication Data

Names: Klepeis, Alicia, 1971- author.
Title: The Tennessee Titans / by Alicia Z. Klepeis.
Description: Minneapolis, MN : Bellwether Media, 2024. | Series: Epic. NFL team profiles | Includes bibliographical references and index. | Audience: Ages 7-12 | Audience: Grades 2-3 | Summary: "Engaging images accompany information about the Tennessee Titans. The combination of high-interest subject matter and light text is intended for students in grades 2 through 7".- Provided by publisher.
Identifiers: LCCN 2023021982 (print) | LCCN 2023021983 (ebook) | ISBN 9798886874969 (library binding) | ISBN 9798886876840 (ebook)
Subjects: LCSH: Tennessee Titans (Football team)--History--Juvenile literature.
Classification: LCC GV956.T45 K54 2024 (print) | LCC GV956.T45 (ebook) | DDC 796.332/640976855--dc23/eng/20230518
LC record available at https://lccn.loc.gov/2023021982
LC ebook record available at https://lccn.loc.gov/2023021983

Editor: Kieran Downs   Designer: Josh Brink

Printed in the United States of America, North Mankato, MN.

TABLE OF CONTENTS

TAKING DOWN A TOP TEAM 4

THE HISTORY OF THE TITANS 6

THE TITANS TODAY 14

GAME DAY! 16

TENNESSEE TITANS FACTS 20

GLOSSARY 22

TO LEARN MORE 23

INDEX 24

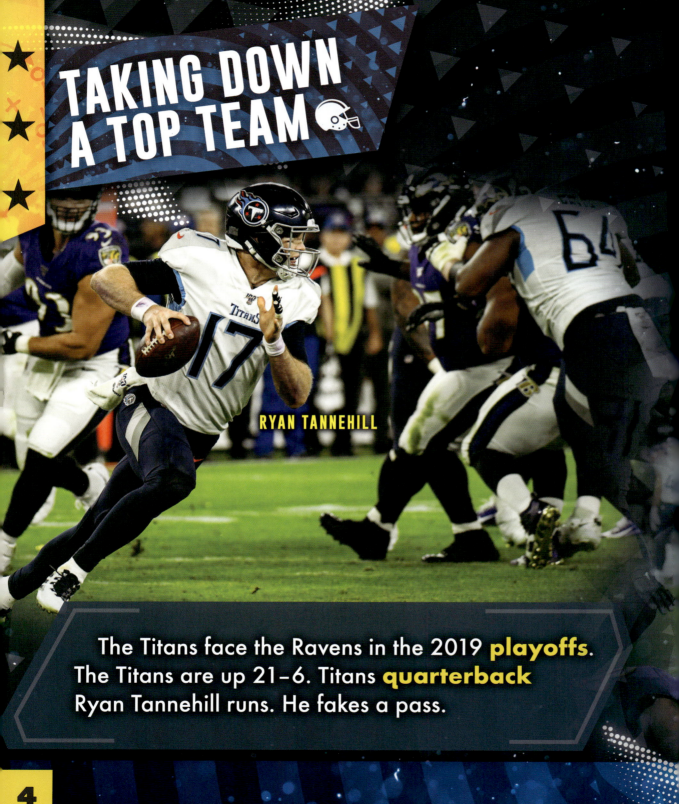

TAKING DOWN A TOP TEAM

RYAN TANNEHILL

The Titans face the Ravens in the 2019 **playoffs**. The Titans are up 21–6. Titans **quarterback** Ryan Tannehill runs. He fakes a pass.

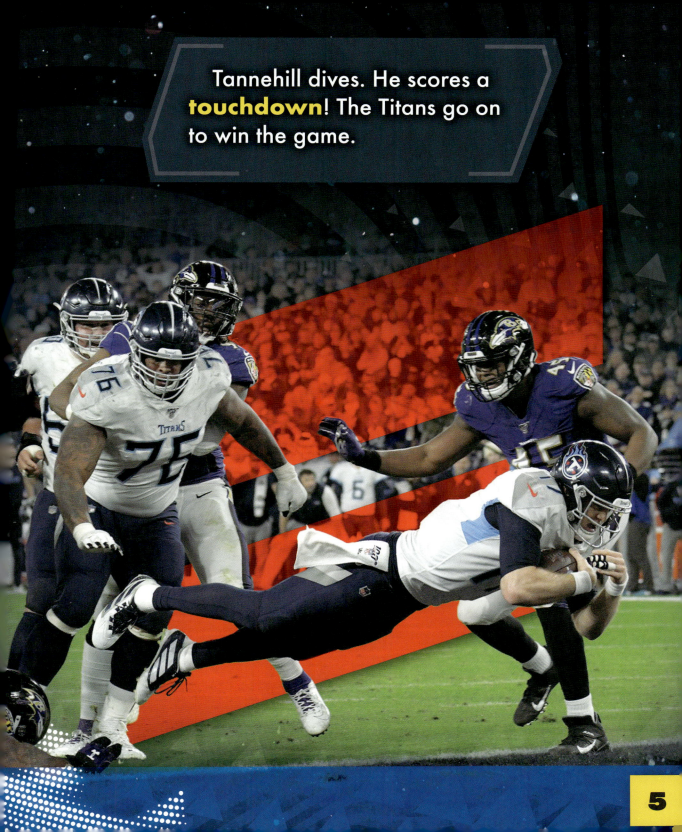

Tannehill dives. He scores a **touchdown**! The Titans go on to win the game.

THE HISTORY OF THE TITANS

The Titans began in Houston, Texas, as the Houston Oilers. They first played in 1960. The team won American Football League (AFL) **championships** in their first two seasons! Star quarterback George Blanda led their winning **offense**.

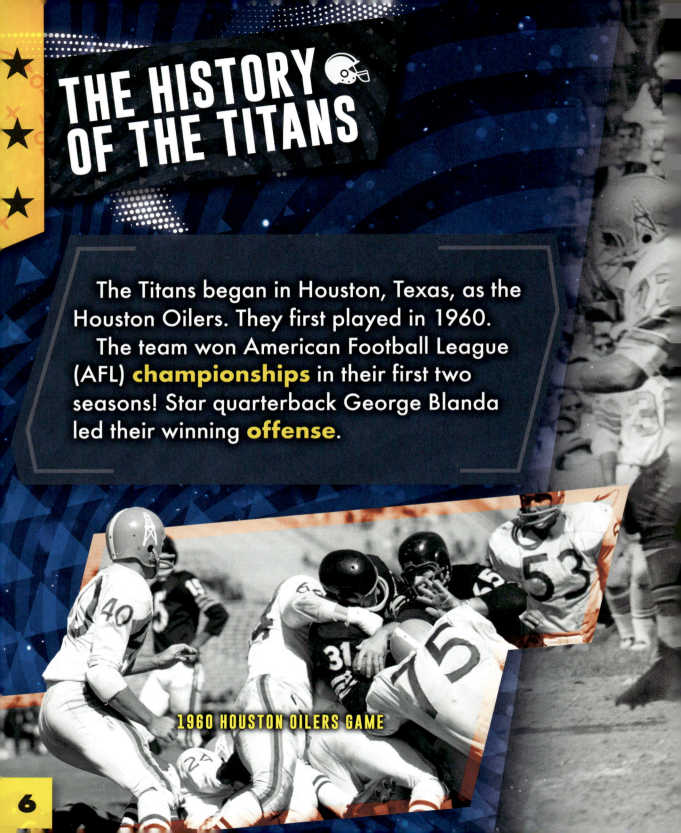

1960 HOUSTON OILERS GAME

GEORGE BLANDA

LONGTIME PLAYER

George Blanda played 26 seasons in the AFL and the National Football League (NFL). He set the record for most years played!

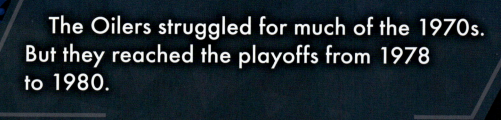

The Oilers struggled for much of the 1970s. But they reached the playoffs from 1978 to 1980.

DIFFERENT LEAGUES

The Oilers were part of the AFL for 10 seasons. They joined the NFL in 1970.

1978 PLAYOFF GAME

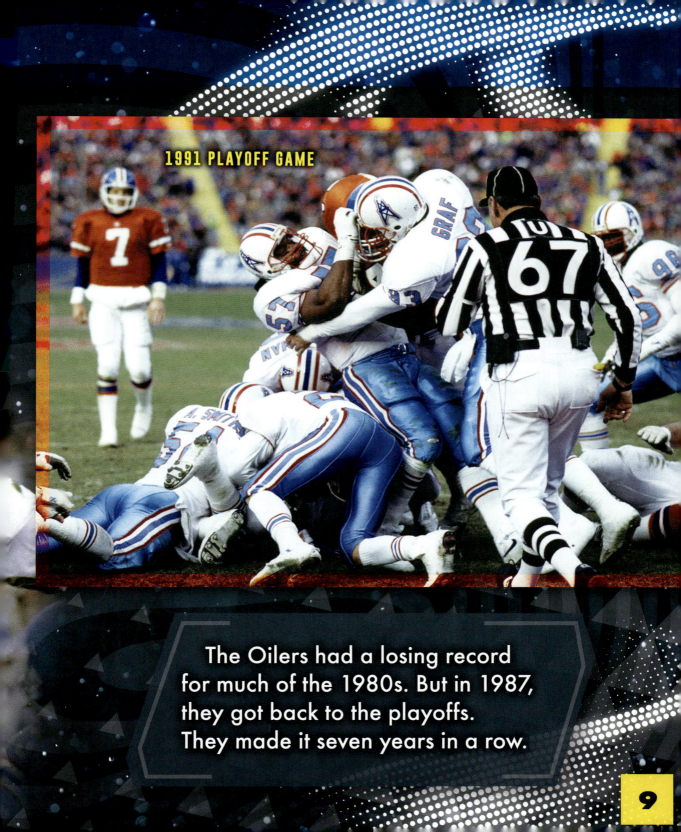

1991 PLAYOFF GAME

The Oilers had a losing record for much of the 1980s. But in 1987, they got back to the playoffs. They made it seven years in a row.

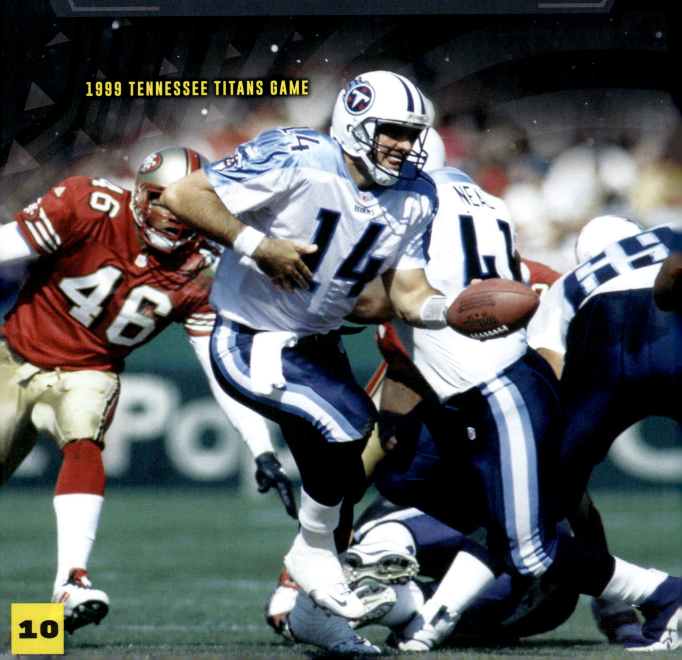

The Oilers started the early 1990s strong. But they never reached the **Super Bowl**. The team traded away many of its star players.

1999 TENNESSEE TITANS GAME

In 1997, the Oilers moved to Nashville, Tennessee. They changed their name to the Titans in 1999.

🏆 TROPHY CASE 🏆

AFC CENTRAL championships
3

AFC championships
1

AFL championships
2

AFC SOUTH championships
4

The Titans reached their first Super Bowl in 2000. But they lost to the St. Louis Rams.

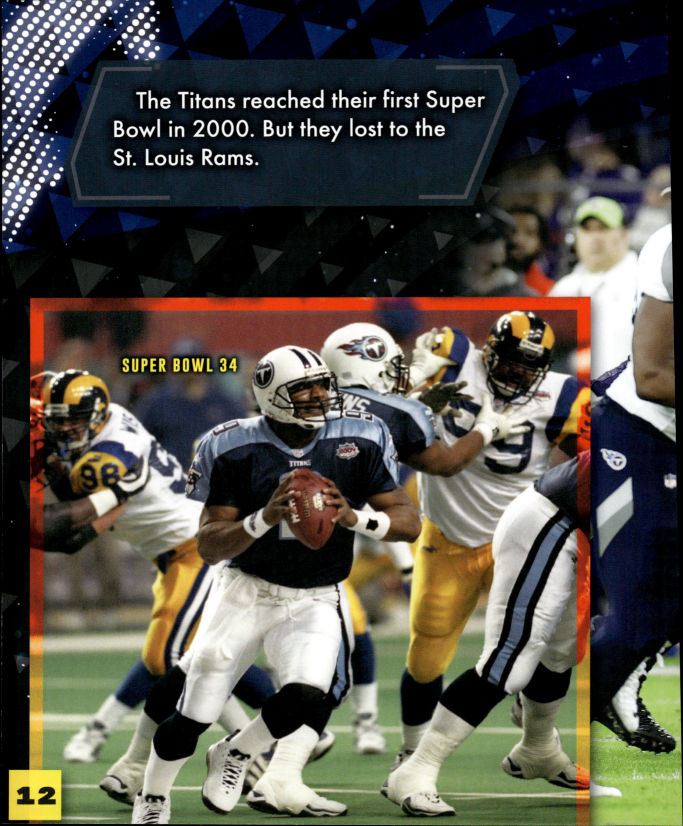

SUPER BOWL 34

DERRICK HENRY

The team struggled for much of the 2010s. In 2016, **running back** Derrick Henry joined the team. He helped the Titans win their **division** in 2020 and 2021.

THE TITANS TODAY

TITANS VS. COLTS

The Titans play their home games at Nissan **Stadium**. It is in Nashville, Tennessee.

The team plays in the AFC South division. One main **rival** is the Indianapolis Colts. The Jacksonville Jaguars are another.

📍 LOCATION 📍

NISSAN STADIUM
Nashville, Tennessee

TENNESSEE

N
W   E
S

GAME DAY!

The Titans **mascot** is T-Rac. He often performs with the cheerleaders on game days. He takes photos with fans.

Many fans wear silver and blue clothing. These are the main team colors.

T-RAC

17

"Get Loud (Titan Up)" is the Titans' theme song. It gets fans excited at game time.

The Blue Crew **Drumline** dances and drums to cheer on their team. The Tennessee Titans give it their all throughout the season!

BLUE CREW DRUMLINE

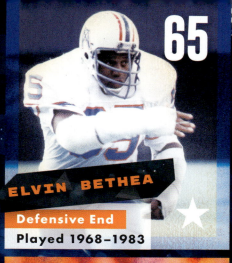

65

ELVIN BETHEA

Defensive End
Played 1968–1983

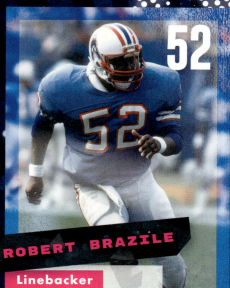

52

ROBERT BRAZILE

Linebacker
Played 1975–1984

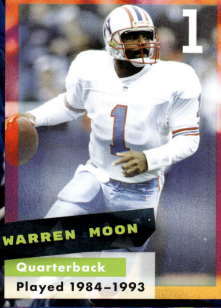

1

WARREN MOON

Quarterback
Played 1984–1993

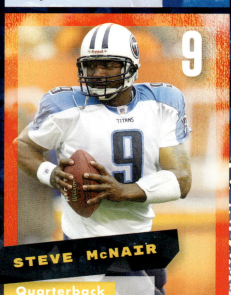

9

STEVE McNAIR

Quarterback
Played 1995–2005

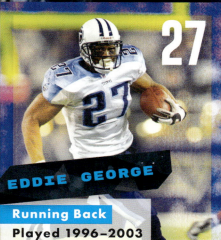

27

EDDIE GEORGE

Running Back
Played 1996–2003

TENNESSEE TITANS FACTS

LOGO

JOINED THE NFL | **1970** (AFL 1960–1969)

MASCOT
T-RAC

NICKNAME | None

CONFERENCE
American Football Conference (AFC)

COLORS

DIVISION | AFC South

Houston Texans

Indianapolis Colts

Jacksonville Jaguars

STADIUM

NISSAN STADIUM
opened August 27, 1999

holds **69,143** people

⏱ TIMELINE

1961
The Oilers win their first AFL championship

1997
The Oilers move from Houston, Texas, to Nashville, Tennessee

2021
The Titans win the AFC South

1970
The Oilers play their first season in the NFL

2000
The Titans play in Super Bowl 34

★ RECORDS ★

All-Time Passing Leader	All-Time Rushing Leader	All-Time Receiving Leader	All-Time Scoring Leader

Warren Moon
33,685 yards

Eddie George
10,009 yards

Ernest Givins
7,935 yards

Al Del Greco
1,060 points

21

GLOSSARY

championships—contests to decide the best team or person

division—a group of NFL teams from the same area that often play against each other; there are eight divisions in the NFL.

drumline—a group of musicians who play drums and cymbals, usually to pump up a crowd

mascot—an animal or symbol that represents a sports team

offense—the group of players who have the ball and try to score

playoffs—games played after the regular season is over; playoff games determine which teams play in the championship game.

quarterback—a player whose main job is to throw and hand off the ball

rival—a long-standing opponent

running back—a player whose main job is to run with the ball

stadium—an arena where sports are played

Super Bowl—the annual championship game of the NFL

touchdown—a score that occurs when a team crosses into their opponent's end zone with the football; a touchdown is worth six points.

TO LEARN MORE

AT THE LIBRARY

Coleman, Ted. *Tennessee Titans*. Mendota Heights, Minn.: North Star Editions, 2022.

Meier, William. *Tennessee Titans*. Minneapolis, Minn.: Abdo Publishing, 2020.

Whiting, Jim. *The Story of the Tennessee Titans*. Minneapolis, Minn.: Kaleidoscope, 2020.

ON THE WEB

FACTSURFER

Factsurfer.com gives you a safe, fun way to find more information.

1. Go to www.factsurfer.com.

2. Enter "Tennessee Titans" into the search box and click 🔍.

3. Select your book cover to see a list of related content.

INDEX

AFC South, 13, 15, 20

AFL championships, 6

American Football League (AFL), 6, 7, 8, 20

Blanda, George, 6, 7

Blue Crew Drumline, 18

colors, 16, 20

famous players, 19

fans, 16, 18

Henry, Derrick, 13

history, 4, 5, 6, 7, 8, 9, 10, 11, 12, 13

Houston, Texas, 6

mascot, 16, 17, 20

name, 6, 11

Nashville, Tennessee, 11, 14, 15

National Football League (NFL), 7, 8, 20

Nissan Stadium, 14, 15, 20

offense, 6

playoffs, 4, 5, 8, 9

positions, 4, 6, 13

records, 7, 9, 21

rivals, 15

Super Bowl, 10, 12

Tannehill, Ryan, 4, 5

Tennessee Titans facts, 20–21

theme song, 18

timeline, 21

trophy case, 11